My Book About

Donald J.

Trump

Tuscawilla Creative Services
CreateTeachInspire.com

For bulk orders, contact info@contacttcs.com.

All photographs in this book are in the public domain and were obtained from WhiteHouse.gov or the Library of Congress.

This publication is a work of humor. It is intended for entertainment purposes only.

ISBN: 978-1-941826-37-9

How to Use this Book

Do you have something to say about Donald J. Trump?

Here's an opportunity to write your book about America's 45th President.

This book includes a mix of lined and blank pages so you can write or draw. It's also illustrated with photos you can write captions for or just use for inspiration.

Not sure what to write? Check the next page for a list of ideas.

Fill in your name on the title page, add a dedication, then turn to page 13 and begin writing.

You can fill in the table of contents as you go or when you've finished.

Finally, if you would prefer that no one else sees these instructions, carefully remove this page from the book. We recommend using an exacto knife.

Now you're ready to proudly display *My Book About Donald J. Trump*.

Need some ideas to help you get started? Write your thoughts on:

- When Donald Trump first announced his candidacy.
- His campaign style.
- His tweets and use of social media.
- Your reaction when he was elected.
- The nicknames he gives his opponents.
- Your life before and after his presidency.
- How he dealt with North Korea.
- How he dealt with Israel and the Middle East.
- Donald Trump and Black Lives Matter.
- How he handled the pandemic.
- His immigration policies.
- His economic policies.
- Donald Trump, the person—husband, father, grandfather, friend, entrepreneur, real estate investor, celebrity.
- His impact on race relations.
- His impact on the standing of the United States in the world.
- The Make America Great Again slogan.
- Donald Trump's campaign rallies.
- The media and fake news.
- The first impeachment.
- The 2020 election.
- The second impeachment.
- Donald Trump's impact on U. S. relations with China.
- The events of January 6, 2021.

My Book About

Donald J. Trump

By

_____

Dedication

_____

_____

_____

_____

_____

_____

_____

_____

_____

_____

_____

Contents

_____

_____

_____

_____

_____

_____

_____

_____

_____

_____

_____

_____

_____

_____

_____

_____

_____

_____

_____

_____

_____

_____

_____

_____

_____

_____

_____

_____

_____

_____

_____

_____

_____

_____

_____

_____

_____

_____

_____

_____

_____

_____

_____

_____

_____

_____

_____

_____

_____

_____

_____

_____

_____

_____

_____

_____

_____

_____

_____

_____

_____

_____

_____

_____

_____

_____

_____

_____

_____

_____

_____

_____

_____

_____

_____

_____

_____

_____

_____

_____

_____

_____

_____

_____

_____

_____

_____

_____

_____

_____

_____

_____

_____

_____

_____

_____

_____

_____

_____

_____

_____

_____

_____

_____

_____

_____

_____

_____

_____

_____

_____

_____

_____

_____

_____

_____

_____

_____

_____

_____

_____

_____

_____

_____

_____

_____

_____

_____

_____

_____

_____

_____

_____

_____

_____

_____

_____

_____

_____

_____

_____

_____

_____

_____

_____

_____

_____

146 | My Book About

_____

_____

_____

_____

_____

_____

_____

_____

_____

_____

_____

_____

_____

_____

_____

_____

_____

_____

_____

_____

_____

_____

_____

_____

_____

_____

_____

_____

_____

_____

_____

_____

_____

_____

_____

_____

_____

_____

_____

_____

_____

_____

_____

"Don't chase people. Be yourself, do your own thing and work hard. The right people – the ones who really belong in your life – will come to you. And stay."

~ *Will Smith*

"I often warn people: Somewhere along the way, someone is going to tell you, 'There is no "I" in team.' What you should tell them is, 'Maybe not. But there is an "I" in independence, individuality and integrity."

- *George Carlin*

"In a survey of 90-year-olds, when asked what they would have done differently, they responded, 'Risk more, reflect more and leave a legacy that matters.'"

- *Dr. Linda Livingstone*
Dean of Pepperdine University Business School

10 Seconds of Inspiration

Get images like these delivered to your inbox every Saturday morning. Enjoy and share!

Visit

CreateTeachInspire.com/ss

to join Shareable Saturday

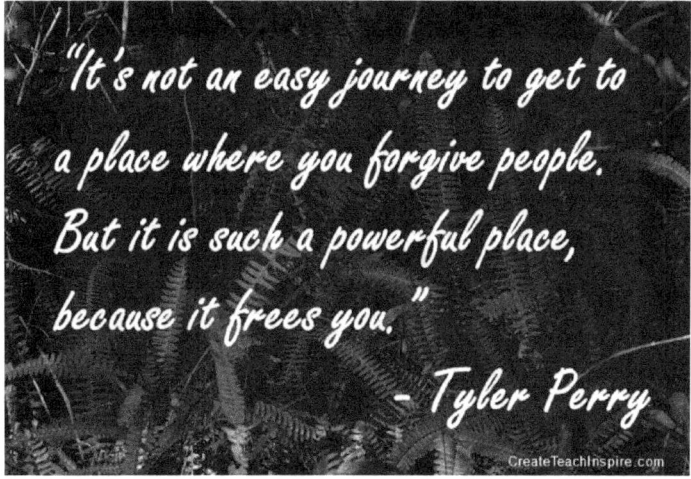

"You cannot get through a single day without having an impact on the world around you. What you do makes a difference, and you have to decide what kind of difference you want to make."

– Jane Goodall

CreateTeachInspire.com

"It's not an easy journey to get to a place where you forgive people. But it is such a powerful place, because it frees you."

– Tyler Perry

CreateTeachInspire.com

A great way to wrap up your week!

Visit **CreateTeachInspire.com/ss** to join Shareable Saturday

www.ingramcontent.com/pod-product-compliance
Lightning Source LLC
Chambersburg PA
CBHW050319120526
44592CB00014B/1968